RUDE WORLD

100 Rudest Place Names in the World

ROB BAILEY AND ED HURST

www.rude-world.com

B🌿XTREE

First published 2006 by Boxtree an imprint of Pan Macmillan Ltd
Pan Macmillan, 20 New Wharf Road, London N1 9RR
Basingstoke and Oxford
Associated companies throughout the world
www.panmacmillan.com
www.rude-world.com

ISBN-10: 0-7522-2622-3
ISBN-13: 978-0-7522-2622-4
Copyright © Rob Bailey and Ed Hurst, 2006

9 8 7 6 5 4 3 2 1

A CIP catalogue record for this book is available from the British Library

Designed by Liz Edwards
Colour Reproduction by Aylesbury Studios Bromley Ltd
Printed by CPI Bath

Acknowledgements

For making it possible ...

The many people around the world who have provided us with images, information, ideas and support.

Warm thanks to ...

Ed's mum (for unbounded and unconditional support), Ed's dad (for suggesting that we should aimlessly travel the world hoping to happen upon a place called Arsebügger); Sally Blouet (for being a delightfully frank sounding board and for excellent design advice); Satish (for international support); Dick and Steve at Positive Images in Richmond (for professional imaging with a human touch); Elliott Devivo for a number of suggestions; and Peter (for inspiring Ed to achieve greater things).

Rob's mum (for suggestions for the book, and ensuring that even the most distant relatives got *Rude Britain* for Christmas), Rob's dad for help with Italian names; Alex (for venturing out with his camera); Dan (for Photoshop advice); Amy (for her patience and suggestions during the writing of this book); Anne (for the invaluable driving, research and support – and for understanding that we had to rush through Petting to get to Fucking); Alice (for her help with French names); Ozge (for suggestions about Turkish places); Sam Jordison (for tips on photo searches and various bits of advice); Deborah (for Photoshop advice); those who contacted others on our behalf (including, but not limited to Sacha, Penny and Cameron); Gavin and Karen for their suggestions and all the material that they shared with us for our website; and Amy, the Baptist Minister's daugther, who explained the meaning of 'Fuk' in a Murano glass shop.

Thanks also to ...

Susan Smith, our excellent agent (for highly professional support and pretending to find us amusing); Penny Price and many others at Boxtree (for agreeing to pay us for the second of these noble projects and for making *Rude Britain* a hit); and David & Anna from the PR Office (for advice and excellent publicity).

Along the way ...

Dr George Sik and his mum (for help with Czech meanings and pronunciations, and for his gallant trip to Slutshole Lane, only to find that some rapscallion had stolen the sign), Peter Millar (for making a special trip to photograph Blue Ball Entry), a Prague taxi driver (for answering Ed's questions, while tactfully not asking too many himself).

While we're at it ...

Rob would like to thank Ed for being disorganised and unpredictable, yet still anal about the most banal of things. Ed would like to express his appreciation towards Rob for being a passive-aggressive stress monkcy.

And finally ...

The people who erected the beautiful wind farm near Weener; the woman who quizzically followed Ed around at Bendova; and the Fucking resident who went some distance out of his way to abuse us – the answer to his question is that brains develop very early in the womb, but how they are used varies from person to person.

If we've forgotten anyone, sorry; in our defence, our brains are addled by travel, our bodies stuffed with service station food, our eyes sore from light boxes and computer screens, and our ears battered from requests to shut up about place-name anecdotes.

CONTENTS

47 Wangen & Tuggen

46 Tit

45 Goffart-Straat

44 Come by Chance

43 Buttzville

42 Höfarten

41 Crap Sés

40 Rue Porte Arse

39 Court Cocking

38 Tightwad

37 Condom

36 Climax

35 Pukë

34 Titz

33 Big Bone Lick

32 Beaverlick

31 Shooting Butts Road

30 Rue de Bitche

29 Meat Cove

28 Mount Mee

27 Nobber

26 Mianus

25 Rimsting

24 Muff

23 Titty Ho

22 Töss

21 Weener

20 Knob Lick

19 Dildo

18 Wan King Path

17 Shatton Moor

16 Dingleberry Road

15 Fuk Man Road

14 Pussy

13 Rue de Labia

12 Fingringhoe

11 Kunst-Wet

THE TOP TEN

10 Gobbler's Knob

9 Bastardo

8 Slut

7 Rimmer Avenue

6 Wank

5 Shitterton

4 Cumming Street & Seaman Avenue

3 Felch Road

2 Cunter

1 Fucking

Explanation of the ranking system
The names presented in this book are ranked according to popular perceptions
of rudeness. This was determined by close consultation with a range of scatological,
geographical etymologists and globally renowned arbiters of taste and decency.
These inputs were carefully analysed and weighted to provide a basic ranking.
This was then adjusted in line with the authors' expert judgement.

Authors' note
The names in this book have emerged over centuries from proud and diverse cultures.
We would like to appeal to readers of this book to treat these places with respect;
please accord privacy and peace to the people who live in these locations.

Pictures
This book has been made possible by generous submissions and assistance from a wide
range of people across the world. All images are individually credited apart from those
places photographed personally by the authors.

Further Information
For further information on rude-sounding place names across the world, please visit
www.rude-world.com

INTRODUCTION

We inhabit an increasingly interconnected world, in which people travel, live and work together more closely than ever before. Technology and commerce provide cities across the world with the same shops, brands and pervasive, international English. Meanwhile, pollution, geopolitics and wars affect us all. It is indeed a 'shrinking world'.

Some people fear that we are entering an age in which we all look, speak, behave and think in the same way; others believe that we are seeing a damaging backlash, in which cultures are adopting intolerant, antagonistic positions to try and ensure that they survive the drive to globalisation. Must we choose between a loss of richness and burgeoning conflict?

Set against this background, why are Tit, Butthole Lane and Poopoo Place so important?

Rude-sounding names are very powerful, representing in microcosm the challenges facing the world. They inspire shared merriment, bring people together and foster understanding as people explore one another's languages and histories. Although the things people find funny vary immensely, humour itself is profoundly human. It is our belief that, as we get beyond sniggering at rude-sounding names, and come to take these places seriously, respect and awe at our common humanity will bind us together – perhaps even speeding our progress towards lasting world peace.

For mutual respect and open-mindedness are as vital now as they have ever been, from global geopolitics to everyday human life. By joining *Rude World's* journey through our planet's place-names, we can all play a part in achieving greater harmony. By challenging the view that these names are rude, we develop understanding and respect – not by belittling the differences between people, but rather by exploring and relishing them.

To anyone who thinks that the world's cultural richness is slipping away, go to Fucking and you will learn otherwise. We defy anyone to visit Windpassing, Bastardo and Slut, and say the richness is lost. By the time you reach Climax, we believe you will be convinced.

This book can never be comprehensive, partly because it is based only on names that appear rude to English-speaking people. What about English names that sound rude in Urdu? Ugandan names that seem odd in Icelandic? Aboriginal names that appear unusual to people from China? The number of combinations is enormous and almost infinitely varied.

We would love to explain the origins of the village of Torba in Turkey that appears to Turkish speakers to mean 'scrotum'. Or explore why it is that notices reading 'Soft Verges' seem to French people to be warning of the presence of less-than-virile penises. Or explain why Cascade d'Arse does not in fact mean, as someone has suggested, 'a veritable cascade of arse'.

In the final analysis, this book can only be a bold but small step in a noble and never-ending quest. In further forays, we hope we will one day make it to Le Tampon on the island of Réunion, Cumbum in India, Rectum in the Netherlands and Spurt in Belgium.

Before you turn the page, may we first welcome you to *Rude World* – a brave and respectful journey through the kaleidoscope of names, cultures and languages of the world. Join us on this journey, and together let us foster global understanding and respect, playing a vital part in developing a world that is at once joined together and boundlessly varied.

If you would like to share in the ongoing quest to gather and understand apparently rude place and street names, please visit us at:

www.rude-world.com

Rob Bailey and Ed Hurst

POOPOO PLACE

100

OAHU, HAWAII: STREET

Situated on the Island of Oahu in Hawaii, Poopoo Place is popular with walkers and tourists.

The name is likely to be connected to the Hawaiian word 'poopoo', which means 'sunken' (as in the eyes of an ill person), 'indented' (as a bay or an inlet from the sea is) or 'a nook and cranny'. Thus the name appears to reflect the secluded and craggy nature of the place.

Photo: Anna www.annazurichini@blogspot.com

Photo: Judy Roenke, www.flickr.com/photos/roenke47

PEEPEE FALLS STREET 99

WAILUKU RIVER STATE PARK, HAWAII: STREET

This street is named after Peepee Falls, a popular waterfall in Hawaii, just above an area of rapids called Boiling Pots.

The word 'peepee' has various meanings in Hawaiian. It can refer to the act of hiding in a tree (in the manner of an owl); it is a type of seaweed; it is the name of a mysterious, ancient illness. Therefore, the name is likely to indicate that this place may be a good hiding place, could be associated with seaweed or have been associated with an illness.

ARS EN RÉ

98

POITOU-CHARENTES, FRANCE: PLACE

Situated in southwest France, Ars en Ré has a long history rich in religious and ecclesiastical connections.

RAMPANT HORSE STREET 97

NORFOLK, ENGLAND: STREET

Situated in Norwich, Rampant Horse Street was named after a pub of the same name, which had previously been called The Ramping Horse. The pub was located near a horse market and was demolished circa 1900.

Thus, the name may simply refer to horses in the area. However, it may also be influenced by the terminology of heraldry and coats of arms, in which animals depicted in an upright position (as they often are on pub signs) are described as 'rampant'.

BUMPASS HELL

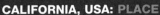

96

CALIFORNIA, USA: PLACE

Situated at Lassen Volcanic National Park in northern California, Bumpass Hell is a collection of geothermic features.

It was named after an explorer named Kendall Bumpass, who discovered the dangers of the place in the 1860s when he fell through the brittle earth into a near-boiling spring below, causing him to lose a leg. The springs give the place a distinctive, sulphurous smell resembling rotten eggs.

PRINCE ALBERT 95

WESTERN CAPE, SOUTH AFRICA: PLACE

Prince Albert is a South African village in the Karoo, part of the Western Cape.

Adjoining the Swartberg Mountains, the original settlement was called Albertsberg after the founder but was later changed, in honour of Queen Victoria's husband, Prince Albert. In common with many places in the region, there was a brief gold rush here in the nineteenth century, but it led to very little success.

One of the most notable structures in the village is the Old Water Mill, which was recently declared a National Monument. The town can also boast a unique architectural feature, the Prince Albert Gable – a particular kind of Dutch-style gable that is only found in this town.

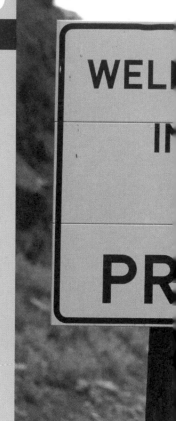

BACK PASSAGE

94

Photo: Nick Small, www.myspace.com/nicksmall

LONDON, ENGLAND: PASSAGEWAY

Situated in the City of London, close to Smithfield Market and the Barbican, this obscure little alleyway is passed by thousands of people each week, yet most people remain unaware of its existence. It seems strange that so functional and secluded a place should have been named at all, but such idiosyncrasies are testament to the rich history of London.

The name 'Back Passage' simply derives from the fact that this is a passageway running around the back of a row of buildings to allow access to their rear entrances.

POO

93

CANTABRIA, SPAIN: PLACE

Poo is situated on the dramatic Atlantic Cantabrian coast of Spain, close to the town of Llanes.

The origins of the name may be related to the Poo family.

BREST

92

Brest is a city in the Bretagne region of northwest France, located on the western tip of the Brittany peninsula. It is an important port and houses a naval base.

PEÑÍSCOLA

91

VALENCIA, SPAIN: PLACE

Peñíscola is a town on the Costa del Azahar, on the eastern coast of Spain. This extremely beautiful area is often referred to as 'the Gibraltar of Valencia', and is only joined to the mainland by a narrow strip of land.

TITMAN ROAD   90

NEW JERSEY, USA: STREET

Titman Road is located in the town of Buttzville, New Jersey.

It was named in honour of the Titman family – farmers that lived in the area for almost 200 years.

See also **Buttzville**.

Photo: Christopher Masiello, www.chris-masiello.com

HOOKER STREET   89

COLORADO, USA: STREET

This street is located in Westminster, a suburb of the City of Denver, Colorado. The name is likely to refer to a former resident of the area with the surname 'Hooker'.

This street should not be confused with Hooker Road in Norwich, England, which was described in detail in *Rude Britain*.

HELL

MICHIGAN, USA: PLACE

Hell was first settled in 1838 by George Reeves and his family. George built a mill and a general store on the banks of a river that is now known as 'Hell Creek'.

There are two main theories to explain the name. The first of these suggests that two German travellers, passing through the area, left their stagecoach, and one said to the other, 'So schöne hell'. 'Hell' in German, means 'bright and beautiful'. Their comments were overheard by locals. When George Reeves was asked what he thought the town should be named, he reportedly replied, 'I don't care, you can name it 'Hell' if you want to.' The name stuck.

The other theory is connected to the area's history as part of the Dexter Trail, a route for transporting goods, which joined Lansing and Dexter, Michigan. The area in which Hell exists is swampy and populated by mosquitoes, making it one of the least pleasant parts of the route. Consequently, it is said that regular travellers dubbed the area 'Hell'.

Photo: Bob Davidson, www.flickr.com/photos/oybay

KNOBS FLAT

SOUTH ISLAND, NEW ZEALAND: PLACE

Situated in the Eglinton Valley, halfway between Te Anu and Milford Sound, Knobs Flat is towered over by majestic mountains. It is in the heart of Fiordland National Park in southwest New Zealand. The area is richly diverse in flora and fauna, boasting alpine meadows, beech forest, kaka, kea, falcon, rock wren, blue duck and bats.

The name may refer to a former resident of the area with the family name 'Knob', whilst the word 'flat' indicates that this is a level area in a place that is predominantly mountainous.

Photo: Jamie Deeman

HORN

ST GALLEN, SWITZERLAND: PLACE

Situated on the shores of Lake Constance, Horn has given its name to various local establishments, such as the Bad Horn Hotel.

The name may owe its origins to the German word 'horn', which has the same meaning as in English (i.e. referring either to a musical instrument or a bony protuberance from an animal's head).

DICKEN 85

ST GALLEN, SWITZERLAND: PLACE

Situated in St Gallen, Dicken is found on a lofty hillside location, reached by carefully negotiating a sereies of hairpin bends.

The name is derived from a German phrase meaning 'a plot of land that is overgrown'. This phrase is associated with the German word 'Dickicht', meaning 'copse' or 'thicket'.

WANG

WIESELBURGER LAND, AUSTRIA:
PLACE

Situated in the northeast of Austria, Wang is only a short drive from one of the four Austrian settlements know by the name 'Windpassing'.

The name may be related to the German word 'wang', meaning 'cheek', perhaps alluding to a local geographical feature shaped like a cheek.

See also **Wangen** and **Wangerland**.

PRUDENT PASSAGE

83

Located close to St Paul's Cathedral, and butting onto Trump Street, it would be very easy to miss this short, dark passage.

The origins of the name are obscure, though the name may be associated with banking and finance. It has been in use since 1875 when it lost its original name of 'Sun Alley'. The passage is lined with white glazed bricks which gives it a clean, clinical feel.

BOTTOM ROAD

82

VALENCIA, SPAIN: STREET

Situated in the Nevada town of Fallon, Bottom Road is probably so-named simply because it runs through the lowest lying part of the area.

This photograph was taken during a round-the-world trip on recumbant bicycles, which explains why the gentleman's helmet is clearly visible in the picture.

Photo: Jim Dowling

SHAG HARBOUR

81

NOVA SCOTIA, CANADA: PLACE

Shag Harbour is located on the east coast of Canada in Nova Scotia. The name is probably a reference to the shag, a common seabird indigenous to many parts of the world, including Canada.

In 1967, Shag Harbour became famous for allegedly receiving a visit from an alien probe. However, in common with most such stories, it has proved impossible to document beyond doubt.

See also **Shag Point**.

CHAPEL HILL MUSEUM
SHAG HARBOUR
TE OF 1967 UFO VISIT

1 km

Photo: William Klos, www.flickr.com/photos/wjklos

SHEPHERD'S BUSH

80

Situated in west London, Shepherd's Bush is a vibrant community hosting a major concert venue, BBC studios and countless hotels. It is one of only a few instances of a place having two identically named, but unconnected, London Underground stations.

The name is likely to refer to the character of the place in years gone by, when it was rural and frequented by shepherds.

SALUBRIOUS PASSAGE

79

SWANSEA, WALES: PASSAGEWAY

Salubrious Passage is a small alleyway in Swansea, butting onto Wind Street in an area once frequented by the charismatic Welsh author Dylan Thomas. It probably dates from the eighteenth century, but could be even older, as Wind Street itself is medieval in origin. It may once have led to a courtyard, with the current thoroughfare being merely a fragment of the original passage.

The name is simply a description of the place as it was when it was named, indicating that it was regarded as pleasant, clean and healthy. In recent years, it had become somewhat dilapidated, prompting refurbishment work in 2003.

Photo: www.beautphotcs.com

PILBARA IRON

← PARKER POINT

EAST INTERCOURSE ISLAND →

OVERLENGTH VEHICLE CROSSING

EAST INTERCOURSE ISLAND

78

WESTERN AUSTRALIA, AUSTRALIA: ISLAND

Situated in Western Australia, East Intercourse Island houses a port serving the nearby iron ore mines.

There is also a corresponding West Intercourse Island.

WANKUM

77

Located on the A2 autobahn, close to the border with the Netherlands, this quiet place is set among flat, agricultural land.

The name may be related to the German verb 'wanken', meaning 'to wobble when drunk', perhaps suggesting a colourful history associated with alcohol.

In addition, the name may have been influenced by the Swiss-German phrase 'keinen Wank tun', meaning 'not to lift a finger', which may suggest that this is regarded as a relaxed or lazy place.

See also **Wank**.

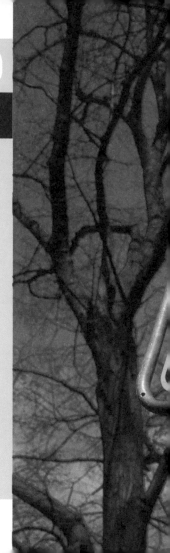

BIG BEAVER ROAD 76

MICHIGAN, USA: STREET

Located in Michigan, Big Beaver is accessed via Big Beaver Road from Exit 69 of Interstate 75 (a main highway in the area).

The name is likely to have French or Native American origins, and to have become corrupted over the years. It may also have been influenced by the prevalence of beavers in the area.

See also **Beaverlick**.

PETTING

75

Petting is a small municipality in Bavaria, Germany. It is located on the shore of a lake called Waginger See.

The earliest recorded reference to this place dates from the year 1048, using the name 'Pettinga'. However, there is some indication that its history extends as early as Roman times.

The meaning of the name is similar to the word 'petting' in English, alluding to a relatively minor act of amorous, physical contact.

WINDPASSING

LOWER AUSTRIA, AUSTRIA: PLACE

Located next to Mauthausen, a place infamous for its World War II concentration camp, Windpassing is a flat and linear settlement, as the bulk of the buildings flank the main road that runs through it.

The name simply refers to the fact that this place is frequently windy, due to its exposed position.

Windpassing should not be confused with several other places of the same name, also in Austria.

HORNÍ STROPNICE

73

Located just inside the Czech Republic's border with Austria, Horní Stropnice is first recorded as having existed in the year 1259. It is on the Stropnice River in the southwest of the country, about five kilometres southwest of the town of Novéhrady.

Its name is somewhat difficult for the native English speaker to pronounce. A phonetic spelling would approximate to 'whore-knee strop-knee-say', though the sound at the beginning of the 'knee' syllable is more akin to the sound at the start of the Russian word 'nyet', meaning 'no'.

The word 'Horní' simply means 'upper', indicating that this is the higher of the two settlements of Stropnice; there is also a place called Dolní Stropnice, the word 'Dolní' meaning 'lower'.

Although 'Stropnice' means nothing directly, the word 'strop' means 'ceiling', so it is likely that the name means 'upper village of somewhere already considered pretty high up' – perhaps as if it is at the ceiling of the world.

See also **Horní**.

THONG 72

KENT, ENGLAND: PLACE

Thong is a village in Kent between Chatham and Gravesend.

The name simply means 'narrow strip of land', and should not be confused with the village of Upperthong, which was discussed in detail in the book *Rude Britain*.

Gland

GLAND

NYON, SWITZERLAND: PLACE

Gland is a town in the district of Nyon in Switzerland. French is the main language spoken there, but over 80 different nationalities are known to live in the vicinity. It is equidistant between the major cities of Geneva and Lausanne, so a range of international companies and organisations have bases here, including the World Conservation Union (IUCN) and the Worldwide Fund for Nature.

Gland can trace its origins back to prehistoric times. The name originated in the Roman period, when a farm called Villa Glanis (meaning 'house of Glanis') was here; 'Glanis' is likely to have been the family name of the owner of the farm. In keeping with these agricultural origins, Gland was a small farming community until the 1960s. However, the opening of the highway linking Geneva with Lausanne attracted commuters to this quiet place, changing its character radically.

SPITAL 70

WALDVIERT, AUSTRIA: PLACE

Situated very close to the Czech border, adjacent to Schagges, this village nestles under a verdant hill. It is typical of small Austrian villages: it is well-tended, clean and orderly.

The name simply derives from an archaic word meaning 'hospital', referring to an institution that was based here centuries ago.

SWALLOW

69

LINCOLNSHIRE, ENGLAND: PLACE

Situated between the Lincolnshire towns of Caistor and Grimsby, Swallow is a small village with a long history. The name may derive from the Anglo-Saxon word 'swalwe' meaning 'rushing stream'.

THE DICKER 68

EAST SUSSEX, ENGLAND: PLACE

The Dicker is located twelve miles from Eastbourne, and is closely associated with the nearby villages of Upper Dicker and Lower Dicker.

There are two credible theories to explain the origins of the name. One relates to the village's history as a centre of local trade – with travellers 'dickering' (bartering) their wares with local tradesmen.

The other explanation is based on the belief that a settlement in the area was built on a plot of land, for which 10 iron rods were paid as rent; this association with the number 10 led to the place being called Decker (from the Middle English word 'dyker', meaning 'ten' – related to the Latin word 'decem'). This name in turn evolved to become Dicker.

For a description of Upper Dicker, please see *Rude Britain*.

MIDDELFART

67

FUNEN, DENMARK: PLACE

Middelfart is a place in central Denmark, located on the island of Funen. Close by is a large bridge over the Little Belt sea strait.

Middelfart is served by the rail service between Copenhagen and mainland Denmark.

The name simply means 'middle passage', referring to one of the three ferry links formerly connecting the island with the peninsula of Jutland.

Photo: Hans Splinter, www.flickr.com/photos/archeon

WINDHAG

66

This Austrian village is not for sufferers of vertigo. Surrounded by mountains and accessed via a steep, winding road, Windhag is located high up on a hill, and hence is frequently windy. The word 'hag' is an old German word meaning 'hedge' or 'grove'. Thus, the name translates as 'windy grove' or perhaps 'windy hedged area'.

HORNÍ 65

PRAGUE, CZECH REPUBLIC:
STREET

Nestling in a quiet corner of Prague, relatively close to the city centre, Horní is an unremarkable, residential street. At the end of the road is a shop prominently advertising the Czech lager, Budweiser Budvar, which has been brewed since 1265 (not to be confused with the American lager, Budweiser).

The word 'horní' simply means 'upper' or 'higher', referring to the elevated position of the road.

See also **Horní Stropnice**.

PÖRNBACH 64

Situated in southern Germany, Pörnbach is a town with an industrial feel.

Pörnbach once belonged to the Counts of Toerring-Gronsfeld, who lived in Toerring Schloss (castle); this structure is first recorded as having existed in 1558. However, since the middle of the eighteenth century, the family have not lived there. The brewery belonging to the castle still produces a range of alcoholic and non-alcoholic drinks.

The component 'Pörn' appears not to translate, simply being a local name. The component 'bach', meaning 'stream', denotes a nearby watercourse. Thus, the name translates as 'the Stream of Pörn'.

BLUE BALL ENTRY 63

HULL, HUMBERSIDE, ENGLAND: STREET

Situated in Hedon, near Hull, Blue Ball Entry is a little street hosting a shop selling blinds and awnings. Facing it is the Hedon Tackle & Bait Shop.

km An Óige

9 LOO BRIDGE

LOO BRIDGE

Situated in Clonkeen, near Killarney, Loo Bridge plays host to a bar and disused railway station (that for many years served as a youth hostel, or 'An Óige' in Irish). This is by no means an uncommon sight, as the once-extensive network of railways in Ireland was decimated in the 1950s and 1960s.

MAKAPIPI ROAD

61

HANA-MAUI, HAWAII: STREET

Makapipi Street is named after the place of the same name, which is known for its scenic splendours.

Nearby are Makapipi Falls and Makapipi Stream. Although the force of the water in this stream has always varied according to rainfall, there is some evidence that its strength is being seriously diminished by human intervention.

In Hawaiian, the word 'maka' has a range of meanings, one of which is 'point of a fish hook'; 'pipi' also has various interpretations, the most likely of which is 'Hawaiian pearl oyster'. Thus the name 'Makapipi' may refer to fishing for pearls.

Photo: Mike Haber

STINKING CREEK ROAD

60

Stinking Creek Road, between Jellico and Duff, is near the rural area of the same name.

Situated in the Cumberland Mountains, Tennessee, Stinking Creek was originally called Sugar Creek because of an abundance of sugar maple trees. The early settlers to the area would harvest maple sap from the trees and boil it down to make syrup and alcoholic drinks.

During the unusually harsh winter of 1779–80, many of the local

farm animals perished. Overwhelmed by the scale of the disaster, the farmers and settlers found it very difficult to deal properly with the carcasses of the animals, many of which were simply dumped into the nearby creek. When the warmer weather of spring arrived, they started to rot, causing a foul smell that recurred for years, and eventually caused the name of the place to be changed.

HOFACKER-STRASSE

BÜTSCHWIL, ST GALLEN, SWITZERLAND:
STREET

Situated in the town of Bütschwil in Switzerland, this street adjoins an industrial estate.

The name simply comprises three elements: 'hof' refers to a farm or courtyard; 'acker' means 'field'; 'strasse' means 'street'. Thus, the name probably translates as 'farm field street'.

MORÓN DE LA FRONTERA

58

Morón de la Frontera is a Spanish town in Andalusia, 63 kilometres southeast of Seville. It is at the point where the flatlands and the hills of the Sierra Sur meet, and is located in a popular tourist area.

This place was formerly known as 'Arunci', a name attributed to the Romans. However, it has been known as 'Morón' since the third century. The word 'Morón' may derive from the Moorish influences in the region; the phrase 'de la Frontera' indicates that it is near the frontier or border with a neighbouring province.

The area is known for the cultivation of olives and cereal crops, providing a contrast to the many manor houses, palaces, churches and ancient convents.

In modern times, Morón is best known for its American airbase. It is not to be confused with Moron in the Jura Mountains of Switzerland, or the Moróns in Argentina and Cuba.

DONG 57

Situated close to Neukirchen-Vluyn, this tiny hamlet is agricultural in character. It is traversed by winding lanes and is bordered by fields containing livestock and a windmill.

This peaceful atmosphere contrasts quite sharply with the modern autobahn (or highway) which passes nearby, carrying heavy traffic at high speeds.

FRENCH LICK

56

INDIANA, USA: PLACE

Photo: Cindy Seigle

French Lick is a town located in Orange County, Indiana, famous for its springs, large hotel and casino.

French Lick was first settled more than 200 years ago by French traders. The surrounding valley was known as 'The Lick' after the discovery of rich mineral springs, which attracted animals that came to lick the salt deposits left on the rocks, and thus boost their mineral levels. The French had plans to exploit the salt deposits commercially; however, in 1803 Napoleon relinquished claims on this area and the French abandoned their trading posts at The Lick. British settlers subsequently arrived and eventually succeeded in establishing a permanent fort against much opposition from the indigenous population.

In more modern times, Franklin D. Roosevelt won his nomination to run for president inside the French Lick Springs Hotel.

BUTTS WYND 55

ST ANDREWS, FIFE, SCOTLAND: STREET

This historic street is located in St Andrews, Scotland, a city that is best known for its university and golf course.

The street owes its name to archery. In Scotland, there was once a requirement for all able-bodied men to be able to bear arms in times of war. To facilitate this, archery ranges were set up, the one in St Andrews being called Bow Butts (or simply the Butts). Although this has since disappeared, its memory lives on in this street name.

'Wynd' is a Scots word for a thoroughfare that usually consists of a narrow path running between buildings to connect two major roads. Because wynds frequently join streets that are at quite different heights, they are frequently regarded as ways up or down hills. In contrast to connotations of the English word 'wind', there is no suggestion that wynds need be curved.

See also **Shooting Butts Road**.

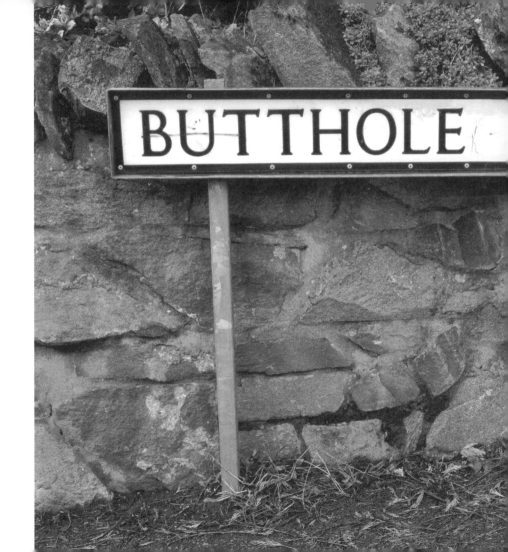

BUTTHOLE LANE

54

Close to the M1 motorway in Leicestershire, this lane begins as a tarmac road in a residential area, but quickly becomes a country byway through farmland. This rural calm is punctured only by the necessity of crossing the motorway.

Although the precise origin of the name is unclear, it seems likely that it is related to an ancient water source – which were always so crucial to the siting of settlements.

FONDAMENTA DE CA LABIA

Situated in Venice, this street runs alongside grand buildings and elegant waterways.

The name comprises a number of elements. 'Fondamenta' refers to a reinforced, artificial water edge of a type common in Venice; it is made by driving stakes made of pine into the ground, and then capping them with stone. The closest equivalent word in English is 'quay', but a fondamenta is not necessarily used to land or moor boats.

'De' simply means 'of', whilst 'ca' means 'house'.

Finally, 'Labia' refers to the name of an affluent family, originally from Spain, who used their wealth to establish themselves in Venetian society in the seventeenth century. They commissioned the nearby Palazzo Labia, a large, ornate building erected at the beginning of the eighteenth century.

Thus the name loosely translates as

Photo: Sabrina Rastelli

53

'quay of the house of the Labia Family', though without any suggestion that boats necessarily land or moor there.

It is said that, in an extravagant display of opulence, one Labia family member sought to impress party guests by throwing a gold dinner service into the canal and declaring 'L'abia o non l'abia, saró sempre Labia', meaning 'Whether I have it or whether I have it not, I will always be a Labia.'

See also **Rue de Labia**.

FANNY 52

QUEBEC, CANADA: STREET

Fanny is a thoroughfare within Fanny Lake campsite in Quebec. It is located in the Jones Springs Area, on the western edge of the Nicolet National Forest. This remote and primitive site is likely to appeal to keen campers with a taste for quiet places.

The surrounding area is rich in wildlife, ranging from fish to turtles, eagles, hawks, foxes, bears and the occasional beaver.

Photo: Andrew Louis

WANGERLAND

51

Wangerland is a Gemeinde (or municipality) in the district of Friesland, Lower Saxony, Germany. It is situated on the North Sea coast, approximately 20 kilometres northwest of Wilhelmshaven. The main village in Wangerland is Hohenkirchen.

This area is largely peaceful, the countryside being characterised by open farmland. There is also an extensive coastline, including nudist facilities. The name is likely to be related to the German word, 'Wang', meaning 'cheek'.

See also **Wang** and **Wangen**.

SHAG POINT

SOUTH ISLAND, NEW ZEALAND: PLACE

Situated in Otago on the South Island of New Zealand, Shag Point is surrounded by geographical features with related names, such as Shag River and Shag Valley. It is likely that the name is simply related to the shag, a very prolific sea bird indigenous to many parts of the world, including New Zealand.

See also **Shag Harbour**.

Photo: Emmanuel Ackaouy

BENDOVA 49

PRAGUE, CZECH REPUBLIC: STREET

Situated on the western fringes of the beautiful, historic city of Prague, Bendova is a quiet street in a residential area. It is dominated by modern, concrete tower blocks and a school, showing clear signs of the time when the country was under Communist control.

By sharp contrast to the prosaic nature of the place, the name simply derives from the Benda family, a dynasty which has for centuries produced composers, conductors and musicians.

SHAFTER 48

CALIFORNIA, USA: PLACE

Shafter, a place in Kern County, is in the Bakersfield Metropolitan Area. The area hosts a variety of industries, notably the manufacturing of concrete pipes. It is also home to the producers of a range of fruit, vegetables and nuts.

Photo:: Patrick Crowley, www.flickr.com/photos/mokolaos

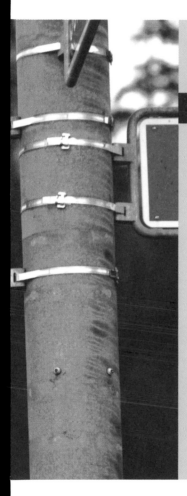

WANGEN & TUGGEN

47

Situated in the Swiss canton of Schwyz, these places are close neighbours.

'Wangen' is simply the German word for 'cheeks'. 'Tuggen', does not translate directly, but may be related to a range of words meaning 'good' or 'virtuous'.

See also **Wang** and **Wangerland**.

TIT

46

TIDIKELT, ALGERIA: PLACE

Situated in southern Algeria, Tit is a town based around an oasis in the Sahara desert. It was visited by contributor Alec Crawford.

In Alec's own words, 'It was just a place we stopped on our travels across Africa.'

There is a dialect spoken in the vicinity, also called Tit.

Photo: Alec Crawford, www.djalecc.com

Photo: Steven Verhasselt & Wesley Van Den Eede

GOFFART-STRAAT

45

BRUSSELS, BELGIUM: STREET

Situated in central Brussels, this street is likely to have been named in honour of the Goffart family.

The name has been associated with eminent artists and historians.

COME BY CHANCE

Photo: Neil Smith, Fort St John, BC

Come by Chance is a town at the head of Placentia Bay on the Avalon Peninsula. It has a harbour, which can be entered between Adams Head and Come by Chance Point. Nearby is the Bungle Gully Dam, a waterway used for boating, fishing and bird watching.

Originally given the name 'Passage Harbour' in 1612, the name 'Comby Chance' was first recorded in 1706. One theory behind the name is that it is simply a reference to its having been discovered accidentally.

It has also been suggested that the name stems from a significant property in the area, once owned by William Colless, called Come-by-Chance Station. According to this theory, the name stems from the fact that an area of land, that had been overlooked, came by chance to the

44

Colless family at a time when most people believed that all of the land in the area had been allocated to other people.

In the 1970s, Come by Chance took on national importance with the building of a huge oil refinery. After years of financial difficulty and disuse, it was reopened in 1987 and is still operating to this day.

BUTTZVILLE

43

NEW JERSEY, USA: PLACE

Situated in New Jersey, the town of Buttzville was named after Robert Buttz, a settler who ran a hotel and store there.

See also **Titman Road**, which is located in Buttzville.

HÖFARTEN

SCHILTBERG, GERMANY: PLACE

Situated in the south of Germany, Höfarten is a rural settlement close to Allenberg.

The word 'hof' means 'farm' or 'courtyard', while 'arten' may be a corruption of the word 'garten' meaning 'garden'. According to this theory, therefore, the name would originally have meant 'farm garden'.

CRAP SÉS

41

Situated on the road from Chur to the exclusive resort of St. Moritz, 'Crap Sés' is the name given to a modern road tunnel.

The name has its origins in Romansh, one of Switzerland's four national languages. It is the name of the hill through which the tunnel runs, which translates as the 'Rock of Conters'; Conters is a nearby place.

See also **Cunter**.

RUE PORTE ARSE

40

MOISSAC, MIDI-PYRENEES, FRANCE: STREET

Rue Porte Arse is a small street in Moissac, near Toulouse in southwest France. Moissac is known for the Abbaye St-Pierre, a major church built in the Romanesque style. The town, which hosts jazz festivals and classical concerts, is located on the northern bank of a river known as 'Le Tarn'.

The name translates as 'road of the door to Arse' or, more figuratively, 'gateway to Arse'.

COURT COCKING 39

ST IVES, CORNWALL, ENGLAND: STREET

Situated in the picturesque, coastal town of St Ives, Court Cocking is one of a series of quaint, twisting streets and courtyards that surround the waterfront. It was formerly known as 'Porth Cocking', meaning 'beach of small boats'. This is likely to be related to 'cockyn', which were small fishing boats that were once kept here. However, it has also been suggested that there may be a link to the Cocking family.

COURT COCKING

lves
a Co.

Photo: Katie Meier, www.katiemeier.com

TIGHTWAD 38

MISSOURI, USA: PLACE

Tightwad is a settlement located in Henry County, Missouri.

Local legend has it that the village's name stems from an occasion when a local store owner cheated a customer out of 50 cents. Some sources claim the transaction involved a watermelon, others a rooster. The word 'tight' refers to the quality of being mean or greedy, whilst 'wad' often describes a hoard of money.

CONDOM

37

GERS, FRANCE: PLACE

Condom is a historic town in the French département (or county) of Gers, founded in the eighth century. The town developed around its ornate cathedral that was almost destroyed by the Huguenots, disaster only being averted when the locals paid a huge ransom.

Condom lies at the centre of the Armagnac region, other trade centring on flour, grain and timber. A prominent local feature is the River Baise, which adjoins a series of quays that were created to enable the transport of Armagnac to Bordeaux.

CLIMAX

MICHIGAN & MINNESOTA, USA: PLACES

MICHIGAN

Climax (Michigan) is located on the east side of Kalamazoo County, Michigan, in an agricultural area.

The original name for the town was 'Climax Prairie', created by a group of settlers led by Daniel B. Eldred. In 1835 they decided to end (or 'climax' as they put it) their search for a place to live. The name was shortened to 'Climax' in 1874. It was incorporated as a village in 1899.

MINNESOTA

Records suggest that Climax (Minnesota) was founded in 1896, the name deriving from a company that produced chewing tobacco.

There is a settlement in nearby Iowa called Fertile. Local legend has it that when a visitor to Climax sadly lost her life in a road accident, the local newspaper reported the event with the headline 'Fertile woman dies in Climax'. It has not proved possible to verify this story.

PUKË

ALBANIA: PLACE AND DISTRICT

With a population of approximately 35,000 people, Pukë is one of the biggest cities in Albania. Taking into account the accent on the final letter, the pronunciation should be 'pooka', though the accent is commonly omitted in writing.

Pukë is in one of the cleanest and most picturesque regions of Albania, and can be found in a beautiful setting in the north of the country (although, controversially, *National Geographic* is quoted as describing Albania as 'the armpit of Europe'). The holes in the sign are bullet holes.

This photograph was submitted by a helpful clergyman, who wishes to remain anonymous.

Photo: Anon (a generous Clergyman)

TITZ

NORTH RHINE-WESTPHALIA, GERMANY: PLACE

Titz is a peaceful village, bypassed by the nearby main road. Records first refer to its existence in the year 1166.

The name is derived from a Celtic German whose name was Titius, the owner of a big farm in the village. The name gradually evolved, in turn becoming Tizene, Titze and, most recently, Titz.

BIG BONE LICK

33

KENTUCKY, USA: PLACE

BEAVERLICK

KENTUCKY, USA: PLACE

Situated in Kentucky, near Cincinnati, Beaverlick and Big Bone Lick are typical of many thriving communities in this part of the United States of America.

In common with other names containing the word 'lick', these areas have a history of mineral deposits that were rich in salt. Animals would come to places where these deposits were accessible to lick them and top up their mineral intake – leading to these places becoming known as 'salt licks'. Often these places would be named after animals that were most associated with them. Hence Beaverlick was often visited by beavers, and Big Bone Lick was visited, during the Pleistocene era, by mammoths (as indicated by the presence of bones in the vicinity).

Photo: Jay Nungesser

SHOOTING BUTTS ROAD

31

MARTINBOROUGH, NORTH ISLAND, NEW ZEALAND: STREET

Photo: Chris Tse, www.flickr.com/photos/asiaticleague

This street runs through the town of Martinborough, South Wairarapa. The area is bounded on one side by the sea and on another by the Ruamahunga River.

The name suggests a history of shooting in the area, as a 'shooting butt' is a position often screened by earth, stone or wood, from which people would shoot game.

This road should not be confused with the street of the same name in Rugeley, England.

See also **Butts Wynd**.

Photo: Camila Rivera (Cami)

RUE DE BITCHE

30

STRASBOURG, FRANCE: STREET

This Strasbourg street, situated between the historic city centre, the Congress Hall and the European Institutes , is popular with tourists.

The name is likely to refer to the town of Bitche in northeastern France, which has its origins in the old castle that stands on a rock 80 metres above the town; this was formerly known as 'Bytis Castrum'. For many years, the castle gave its name to the Countship of Bitsch, which was originally in the possession of the Dukes of Lorraine.

MEAT COVE

29

NOVA SCOTIA, CANADA: PLACE

Situated on Cape Breton island, Nova Scotia, Meat Cove is a quiet, rural place noted for its beautiful walking trails, woodlands and coastal views. The cove itself is one of a series of inlets and bays in the region.

The name probably derives from the fact that sheep used to graze on the cliffs in this part of the island, and occasionally fall into the sea. The local currents are such that the carcasses tended to stay in the vicinity of the cove, leading to a persistent and unpleasant smell. As a result, the area was avoided for many years, until measures were taken to prevent the sheep from falling off the cliffs.

NOBBER

27

COUNTY MEATH, REPUBLIC OF IRELAND: PLACE

Situated on the eastern side of Ireland, Nobber is a quiet and attractive little town.

The name is a corruption of the Irish name for this place, 'An Obair', meaning 'The Work', which may refer to a Norman fortification previously at the north of Nobber. Archaeologists of the area have been buoyed in recent times by the discovery of several high crosses suggesting that this was once a Christian monastic settlement. This has led some people to hope that there will be a growth in tourism in the area.

MIANUS 26

CONNECTICUT, USA: PLACE

Mianus, a locality in Connecticut, is characterised by a growing town and the Mianus River. This area was

once part of a large woodland, but much of this has been lost, initially to agriculture and now to suburban encroachment. Happily, there is a protected area of ancient forest called the Mianus River Gorge Preserve.

The town of Mianus takes its name from the Mianus River, which was named in honour of the leader of the Wappinger Confederacy, Chief Myanos, who was killed near the Gorge in 1683.

RIMSTING 25

Situated in the south of Germany, Rimsting is a Bavarian village with an unspoilt, rural atmosphere.

There are two explanations for the name. One of these suggests that it originated in the archaic form 'Riminisc', a reference to the historical influence of the Romans in the area. The other suggests that it was founded by someone called Rimisto, whose name evolved into the current place-name.

The first reference to the name Rimsting dates from the year 1180 when it appears in historical records.

MUFF

24

COUNTY DONEGAL, REPUBLIC OF IRELAND AND COUNTY LONDONDERRY, NORTHERN IRELAND: PLACE

Situated primarily in County Donegal, this charming and neatly kept place can be found in both Northern Ireland and Eire, as it straddles the border. The name, which in its original Irish form is 'Magh' (later adapted to 'Mough'), simply means 'plain' – referring to the area's simple appearance. To the east, the town is bounded by Lough Foyle.

TITTY HO

23

RAUNDS, NORTHAMPTONSHIRE, ENGLAND: STREET

Situated in the village of Raunds, you will find Titty Ho adjacent to a garage selling classic cars and a company that services washing machines. The village had a moment of fame in 2003 when it was visited by the Channel Four programme, *Time Team*.

This street name is of obscure origin. The second word may be an abbreviation of the word 'house', perhaps indicating that a significant property was once situated here. The first word may suggest that it was named after local birds or a family with the surname 'Titty'.

TÖSS

22

Situated in northern Switzerland, Töss is an industrial quarter of the town of Winterthur.

The name is likely to share common roots with the nearby River Töss.

WEENER

LOWER SAXONY, GERMANY: PLACE

Weener is a town in Lower Saxony, Germany. It is near the border with the Netherlands, on the river Ems, approximately 10 kilometres southwest of Leer (see inset). The first historical trace of Weener is in monastic records from the year 951. The town was once an important inland port for trading agricultural products and peat. Now, the marina is mostly used by leisure craft and yachts.

The old part of the town is full of houses built in the eighteenth and nineteenth centuries. In 1973, Weener and several other villages merged to make the modern town, which has more than 15,000 inhabitants.

The name 'Weener' may have it origins in the Weener family, a surname that was first found in Austria.

KNOB LICK

20

Situated in Missouri, 'Knob Lick' is a name with interesting origins. The word 'Knob' may be based on the Iroquois Indian word 'Ken-tah-ten', meaning 'land of tomorrow'.

The word 'Lick' refers to a place where salt is found on the surface of the earth, to which wild animals often resort; they lick the salt to replenish their mineral levels. This has caused such places to be termed 'salt licks', which are often, though not invariably, located near to salt springs.

Knob Lick is well known for being a place where the local deer come to replenish their salt. As a result, it was a popular place to hunt deer.

Photo: Nanette and Dan Wells

DILDO

NEWFOUNDLAND, CANADA: PLACE

Situated on the southeastern Dildo Arm of Trinity Bay, Newfoundland, Dildo was settled in the early nineteenth century. Since then, the area has always been associated with fisheries. For decades, there was also significant whaling in the area, though the ban on this activity in the 1970s caused a change in focus to conservation of the whale. Likewise, the mink farms once associated with Dildo have closed.

Every summer, the town sponsors a major community event called Dildo Days which often prove popular.

The origins of the name 'Dildo' may be connected to the place's association with fishing, as it was a traditional word for the two round pegs used in a dory (a small traditional rowing boat) which brace the oars when rowing. There is also some suggestion that the town was named after a location in Spain or Portugal, a variety of tree, or the shape of the headland.

WAN KING PATH

18

Wan King Path is located in the town of Sai Kung, in the east of Hong Kong's Kowloon Peninsula.

The name is likely to be a phonetic spelling of a Chinese word, meaning 'surrounding', suggesting that this street was once on the edges of a community, or perhaps that it is regarded as a secluded place.

It is also possible that the road was named to honour a local family of the same name.

Wan King Path

28←14 灣景街

SHATTON MOOR

17

DERBYSHIRE, ENGLAND: PLACE

Shatton Moor is a beautiful upland area in the High Peak district of Derbyshire, England, approximately 15 miles west of Sheffield.

The two nearby hamlets of Shatton and Brough are friendly rivals, holding numerous sporting competitions each year.

DINGLEBERRY ROAD 16

IOWA, USA: STREET

This street, located in Iowa City, is probably named after a variety of cranberry native to the southeastern part of the United States of America. The southern mountain cranberry (or to give it its botanical names, *Vaccinium erythrocarpum* and *Oxycoccus erythrocarpus*) is popularly known as the 'dingleberry', the 'bearberry' or 'arando'. This deciduous shrub is often to be found in woodlands and blossoms in June, producing hermaphroditic flowers. Later in the year, it produces scarlet berries.

It is likely that this street is located in an area once associated with dingleberry bushes.

Another, less likely, explanation is that that this street was named after a now-defunct brand of confectionery of the same name. They consisted of chocolate balls.

FUK MAN ROAD

15

SAI KUNG, KOWLOON, HONG KONG: STREET

Fuk Man Road is located in the town of Sai Kung, in the east of Hong Kong's Kowloon Peninsula.

The word 'fuk' is the western spelling of the Chinese character meaning 'happiness'; thus the phrase 'fuk man' simply means 'happy people' or 'happy man'.

Despite its somewhat obscure location, you will find the Young Women's Christian Association (YWCA) on Fuk Man Road.

Fuk Man Road
福民路

PUSSY

14

SAVOIE, FRANCE: PLACE

Close to the river Isère and the mountain of Mont Bellachat you will find Pussy.

This village is situated in the Savoie département (administrative area) of France, not far from Moûtiers.

The name derives from the Gallo-Roman name 'Pusiacum', which in turn evolved from the word 'pusus' meaning 'little boy'.

Main Photo: Gerard Hoen, Inset Photo: Robert McHenry

RUE DE LABIA 13

CELLES, LIEGE, BELGIUM: STREET

Situated in a peaceful area of rural Belgium, Rue de Labia is located on the periphery of the village of Celles.

The name is derived from the Latin word 'labia', meaning 'lips'. This usage refers to the banks of a nearby river, simply because such a feature was said to resemble lips. The fields adjoining this road have an interesting history, containing the ruins of ancient tombs.

See also **Fondamente de Ca Labia**.

FINGRINGHOE

12

This lovely village can be found tucked away in a fold of land in Essex, south of Colchester. The name means 'the place on a raised area of land (hoe), looking a little like a finger'.

Towards the middle of the village can be found a military practice area (a small arms range), a post office, a green with a beautifully carved and painted village sign, and Fingringhoe Club. However, Fingringhoe is probably best known for the nature reserve at Fingringhoe Wick where a number of species of bird can be observed including sand martins, turtle doves and nightingales.

KUNST-WET

BRUSSELS, BELGIUM: PLACE

Kunst-Wet is a name given to a station on the Brussels Métro system in Belgium which lies beneath a major road junction. The name derives from the Flemish names of the two streets that meet here. One of these streets is Kunstlaan (known in French as 'Avenue des Arts'), meaning 'Arts Lane'; this street forms part of the city's 'inner ring'. The other street is Wetstraat (known in French as 'Rue de la Loi'), meaning 'Law Street'. Thus Kunstlaan and Wetstraat have been abbreviated and combined to give the name Kunst-Wet – perhaps symbolically representing the incongruous meeting of the arts and the law.

This photograph was submitted by Dr George Sik, who was with a group of friends on a stag weekend, during which they sampled the delights of local beers such as Slag, Bush and Palm Spéciale. He informs us that their route was carefully planned, requiring them to take care not to get off before Kunst-Wet.

Photo: George Sik

THE TOP TEN

WARNING:
DO NOT PROCEED
BEYOND THIS POINT
IF EASILY OFFENDED

GOBBLER'S KNOB

PENNSYLVANIA, USA: PLACE

Gobbler's Knob, a small place approximately two miles east of the town of Punxsutawney, is a wooded hill commanding beautiful views.

It is a place that is very much associated with the traditional North American festival known as 'Groundhog Day' that is celebrated on 2 February. According to the tradition, if an animal known as a groundhog emerges from its burrow on this day and does not see its own shadow because the weather is cloudy, winter is about to end. If the groundhog sees its shadow because the weather is bright and clear, it will be frightened and run back into its hole, indicating that winter will continue for another six weeks.

The word 'gobbler' is an alternative word for a turkey, probably referring to an animal with which this place was once associated. The second part of the name is based on an archaic use of the word 'knob' to denote a hill. Therefore, the name is likely to mean 'the hill of the turkey'.

10

BASTARDO

UMBRIA, ITALY: PLACE

Bastardo is a small town in the Italian province of Perugia, in central Umbria, in the valley of a river called Torrente Puglia. The area is noted for its wheat, olive oil and wine. The town is small and does not have its own mayor or council; nevertheless, it has several hotels and restaurants – a result of the fact that it is located in one of the more scenic areas of Umbria.

The town developed around an inn in the seventeenth or eighteenth century, and was formerly known as 'Osteria del Bastardo', which translates as 'Bastard's Inn'. It has been suggested that the inn was given this name by the locals because it was built and run by someone from outside the local area, who consequently was regarded with some disdain.

9

Photo: Robin K. Blum, In My Book® (www.inmybook.com)

SLUT

8

EKERÖ, SWEDEN: PLACE

In the northeast corner of Sweden, you will find Slut. It is located in Ekerö, close to Stockholm.

'Slut' simply means 'the end' or 'closing' in Swedish, perhaps denoting its distance from other settlements, or its secluded character. In Sweden, shops which are closing down often display notices in the window reading 'Slut Sale', which can cause some confusion.

zon 3 15509

SL

Kyrkan

311 Slut

Photo: Ms. Monica Karlsson

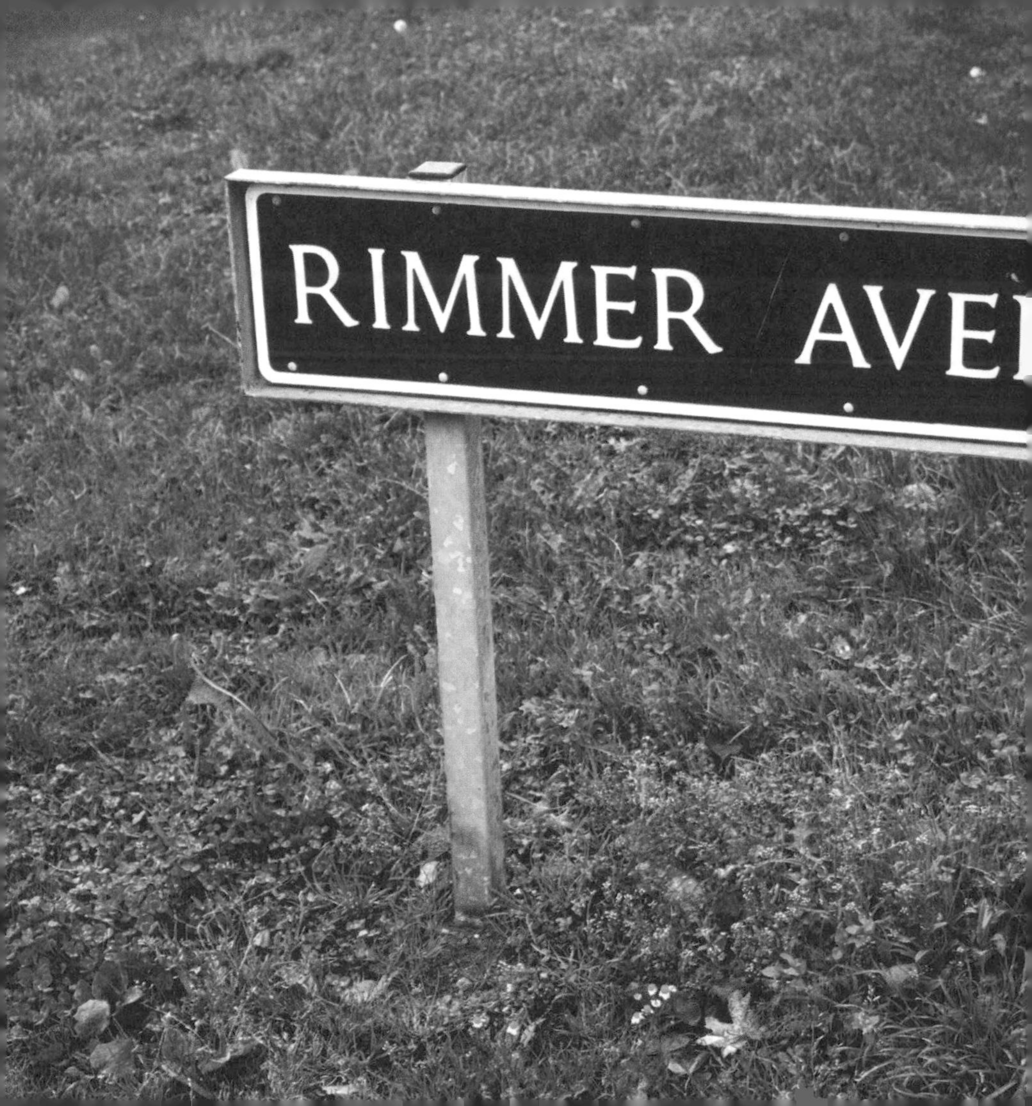
RIMMER AVE

RIMMER AVENUE

HUYTON, MERSEYSIDE, ENGLAND: STREET

Situated in the Merseyside town of Huyton (near Liverpool), Rimmer Avenue is a residential street close to the M62 motorway.

It has been suggested that the street is named in honour of John Thomas Rimmer (1878–1962), who was a British athlete and winner of two gold medals at the 1900 Summer Olympics.

The Rimmer family name has Anglo-Saxon origins, referring to someone who works as a poet; it has the same linguistic roots as the word 'rhyme'.

This street should not be confused with the village of Rimswell, discussed in *Rude Britain*.

7

WANK

BAVARIA, GERMANY: PLACE

Situated in southern Germany, Wank is a small village at the foot of the Wank mountain. Nearby is an inn called Wankhaus.

The name does not directly translate; however, the German verb 'wanken' means 'to wobble when drunk', which may indicate that this place has a colourful history associated with alcohol.

In addition, the name may have been influenced by the Swiss-German phrase 'keinen Wank tun', meaning 'not to lift a finger', which may suggest that this is regarded as a relaxed or lazy place.

See also **Wankum**.

6

SHITTERTON

BERE REGIS, DORSET, ENGLAND: PLACE

Close to Yearling's Bottom, Shitterton is a
hamlet adjoining the Dorset village of
Bere Regis, a short distance away from
Tolpuddle, a place made famous by the
Tolpuddle Martyrs. In the nineteenth
century, these six farm labourers set up
a union to challenge their abject poverty,
and their plight is often held to have played
a major part in the formation of modern-day
trade unionism. Nearby Puddletown (formerly
known as 'Piddletown') was the inspiration for
the fictional town of Weatherbury in Thomas
Hardy's novels.

It has been suggested that the name Shitterton
simply means 'the village on the stream that is
used as an open sewer'.

CUMMING STREET & SEAMAN AVENUE

NEW YORK, USA: STREETS

Situated in Manhattan, New York City, these two streets intersect at a point close to Broadway and Dyckman Street.

Seaman Avenue was named in honour of Henry B. Seaman, whose family owned property west of Broadway from 215th to 217th Streets. Little remains of this vast estate, but a prominent remnant is the Seaman-Drake Arch, a rather neglected landmark in the area. The Seaman family is also known for having introduced the smallpox vaccine into the United States.

Cumming Street was named after another local property owner on 11 May 1925.

FELCH ROAD

FLORHAM PARK, NEW JERSEY, USA: STREET

Located in Florham Park, New Jersey, this road may have been named in honour of Alpheus Felch (1804–96), a figure in early United States history. His grandfather was a veteran of the American Revolutionary War, and Alpheus achieved notoriety in his own right. He became Governor of Michigan, was elected to the United States Senate and served as the president of a commission to settle Spanish and Mexican land claims in California.

Although they may have been named in honour of the same person, there appears to be no direct connection with Felch Township, on Michigan State Highway 69.

3

Photo: Ed Lee

CUNTER

GRAUBÜNDEN, SWITZERLAND: PLACE

Situated in the Albula district of Graubünden, one of the 26 cantons (or states) that make up Switzerland, Cunter is a small community on the road to the Julier Pass.

The name 'Cunter' has its origins in Romansh, one of Switzerland's four national languages. The name simply means 'towards' or 'in the direction of'. In German, the same place is known as 'Conters im Oberhalbstein', meaning something approximating to 'place on the way to the Oberhalbstein mountain range'.

See also **Crap Sés**.

FUCKING

AUSTRIA: PLACE

Fucking is a small, well-tended, but modest Austrian village. It is only a short drive over the border from the German village of Petting.

The name dates back to approximately 1070 and comprises two parts: 'ing' is an old German word meaning 'people'; 'Fuck' comes from 'Focko', the name of an early resident. Hence the name means 'the place of Focko's people'.

The Fucking residents, concerned by the cost of replacing stolen road signs, held a vote in 2004 over the future of the name, but decided to keep it as it is. However, tourists visiting to view the road signs should not expect to be given a warm welcome. By shouting 'pack your bags and go home' at outsiders with cameras, the residents may have missed an opportunity similar to the one seized by the inhabitants of Knockin in Shropshire, UK, who named their general store and post office 'The Knockin Shop'. Although sitting on a potential money-spinner, the Austrian villagers seem to prefer to curse visitors rather than to embrace the potential for selling local memorabilia via a 'Fucking Shop'.

PLACES INCLUDED

Country	State/County/Region	Name
Albania	N/A	Pukë
Algeria	Tidikelt	Tit
Australia	Queensland	Mount Mee
	Western Australia	East Intercourse Island
Austria	Lower Austria	Windpassing
	Upper Austria	Fucking
	Waidhofen	Windhag
	Waldviert	Spital
	Wieselburger Land	Wang
Belgium	Brussels	Kunst-Wet
		Goffart-Straat
	Liège	Rue de Labia
Canada	Newfoundland & Labrador	Come by Chance
		Dildo
	Nova Scotia	Meat Cove
		Shag Harbour
	Quebec	Fanny
Czech Republic	Chko	Horní Stropnice
	Prague	Bendova
		Horní
Denmark	Funen	Middelfart
England	Cornwall	Court Cocking
	Dorset	Shitterton
	Derbyshire	Shatton Moor

Country	State/County/Region	Name
England (continued)	East Sussex	The Dicker
	Essex	Fingringhoe
	Humberside	Blue Ball Entry
	Merseyside	Rimmer Avenue
	Kent	Thong
	Lincolnshire	Swallow
	London	Back Passage
		Prudent Passage
		Shepherd's Bush
	Leicestershire	Butthole Lane
	Norfolk	Rampant Horse Street
	Northamptonshire	Titty Ho
France	Brittany	Brest
	Gers	Condom
	Midi-Pyrénées	Rue Porte Arse
	Poitou-Charentes	Ars en Ré
	Savoie	Pussy
	Strasbourg	Rue de Bitche
Germany	Bavaria	Petting
		Rimsting
		Wank
	Ingolstadt	Pörnbach
	Lower Saxony	Wangerland
		Wecner
	North Rhine-Westphalia	Dong
		Titz
		Wankum

Country	State/County/Region	Name
Germany (continued)	Schiltberg	Höfarten
Hawaii	Hana-Maui	Makapipi Road
	Oahu	Poopoo Place
	Wailuku River State Park	Peepee Falls Street
Hong Kong	Kowloon	Fuk Man Road
		Wan King Path
Italy	Umbria	Bastardo
	Venice	Fondamenta de Ca Labia
New Zealand	North Island	Shooting Butts Road
	South Island	Knobs Flat
		Shag Point
Republic of Ireland (& Northern Ireland)	Clonkeen	Loo Bridge
	County Meath	Nobber
	County Donegal & County Londonderry	Muff
Scotland	Fife	Butts Wynd
South Africa	Western Cape	Prince Albert
Spain	Andalucia	Morón de la Frontera
	Cantabria	Poo
	Valencia	Peñíscola
		Bottom Road
Sweden	Ekerö	Slut
Switzerland	Graubünden	Crap Sés
		Cunter
	Nyon	Gland
	Schwyz	Wangen & Tuggen

Country	State/County/Region	Name
Switzerland (continued)	St Gallen	Dicken
		Hofackerstrasse
		Horn
	Zürich	Töss
USA	California	Bumpass Hell
	California	Shafter
	Colorado	Hooker Street
	Connecticut	Mianus
	New Jersey	Felch Road
	Indiana	French Lick
	Iowa	Dingleberry Road
	Kentucky	Beaverlick
		Big Bone Lick
	Michigan	Big Beaver Road
		Hell
		Climax
	Minnesota	Climax
	Missouri	Knob Lick
		Tightwad
	New Jersey	Buttzville
		Titman Road
	New York	Cumming Street & Seaman Avenue
	Pennsylvania	Gobbler's Knob
	Tennessee	Stinking Creek Road
Wales	Swansea	Salubrious Passage

INDEX